Dale Earnhardt

Remembering the Intimidator

TRIUMPH
B O O K S
CHICAGO

This book is not endorsed or sponsored by NASCAR or its affiliates. This is not an official publication.

Farewell to a Legend

To racing fans, there was no better sight than that of the legendary No. 3 car emerging from the sun-beaten asphalt and onto the back bumper of the leader, tearing around Turn 4 and into first place to the dismay of unsuspecting competitors and to the delight of a roaring crowd. Opponents' views of the menacing black Chevy and its relentless driver were quite different, as seeing The Intimidator approach in the rear-view mirror was enough to justify sweaty palms, lumps in the throat and, more often, full-on panic.

That is how NASCAR followers and drivers will remember Dale Earnhardt, the greatest competitor the sport has ever seen. While fiercely aggressive on the track, he was kind and selfless off of it. Whether you are a veteran fan of the sport of auto racing, or someone who was lured in by the more recent feats of Dale Earnhardt, we hope you find this commemorative issueboth meaningful and enjoyable.

From the editors

Contents

Linc Wonham/Executive Editor
Ray Ramos/Creative Director
Aaron George, Tom Caestecker/Editors
Liz Coats, Don Mastri, Gina Ruffolo/Graphic Designers

Rick Kieras/Imaging Manager
John Orellana/Scanner Operator

The Final Turn

EARNHARDT FOUGHT TO THE END ON A TRAGIC DAY AT DAYTONA

By Jason Wilde

AP/WIDE WORLD PHOTOS

The Turn-4 crash ended Earnhardt's life just moments before the conclusion of his 22nd Daytona 500.

Seconds before the checkered flag on Sunday, February 18, less than half a mile from the finish line, Dale Earnhardt's familiar black No. 3 Chevrolet slammed into the concrete outside retaining wall in Turn 4 of Daytona International Speedway in Daytona Beach, Florida. Suddenly, in the final turn of the final lap of NASCAR's greatest race, the sport had lost one of its greatest legends.

And it will never be the same without him.

Earnhardt's fatal crash cast an enormous pall over what had been one of the most competitive Daytona 500s in the 43-year history of the Super Bowl of stock-car races.

Earnhardt, the driver who had come to define NASCAR, died instantly from massive head injuries.

"Incredible. Just incredible," driver Jeremy Mayfield said. "You figure he'll bounce right back. Your first thought is, 'Hey, he'll probably come back next week at Rockingham and beat us all.'"

That will not happen. The Intimidator is suddenly gone. Those left behind were stunned as word of his death spread. Fans cried, the large American flag in the middle of the speedway's infield was lowered to half-staff.

The Final Turn

Nearly two hours after the race, NASCAR president Mike Helton, his voice cracking with emotion, walked into the infield media center with the news everyone feared.

"This is undoubtedly one of the toughest announcements I have ever personally had to make," Helton said. "We've lost Dale Earnhardt."

Days before the race, Richard Childress, the owner of Earnhardt's Chevrolet, surveyed aerodynamics changes and new restrictions placed on cars by NASCAR and made a prediction. "It's going to be the best Daytona 500 we've ever seen," he said.

Instead, it was the saddest.

Earnhardt was the first driver killed in the Daytona 500, which began in 1959. Six drivers had died of injuries from wrecks during practice or qualifying races for the 500, but never in the race itself. Neil Bonnett, Earnhardt's best friend in racing, was killed in practice in 1994. Rodney Orr died in a wreck three days later, also in practice, and was the last Winston Cup driver killed at the track until Earnhardt's crash. ➔

His journey ended in a most noble way, as Earnhardt fought to secure the victory of team member Waltrip.

An empty victory

Earnhardt was a seven-time Winston Cup champion, and his 76 victories were the most among active drivers. Earnhardt won more races at Daytona International Speedway — 32 — than any other NASCAR driver.

But he'd been the runner-up at the Daytona 500 four times the last eight years and it wasn't until 1998, in his 20th attempt, that he captured the most coveted checkered flag in stock-car racing. In the final race of his career, Earnhardt was credited with 12th place.

"He had what I felt were life-ending type injuries at the time of impact and nothing could be done for him," said Dr. Steve Bohannon, an emergency physician at Halifax Medical Center who also works for the speedway.

Michael Waltrip, the driver Earnhardt thought of as a younger brother, won the race, while his son, Dale Earnhardt Jr., finished second. It should have been the biggest moment in the short history of the Dale Earnhardt Inc. race team, a 1-2 finish at the Great American Race.

Waltrip, the younger brother of recently retired NASCAR star Darrell Waltrip, had spent his entire career struggling in the shadow of his brother, who won 84 races and three

championships. Then, at the end of last season, Earnhardt gave Michael the break he'd been waiting for, hiring him as a teammate of Earnhardt Jr. and Steve Park on the Dale Earnhardt Inc. team. Earnhardt himself, meanwhile, continued to drive cars owned by Childress, his longtime friend.

But for Waltrip, who had been winless during the previous 15 seasons and 462 races in his Winston Cup career, the monumental victory was rendered completely meaningless. When he first reached Victory Lane, Waltrip was overjoyed, shouting, "This is the Daytona 500, and I won it! I won the Daytona 500! I can't believe it!"

But he was somber as it became apparent that his new boss, who gave him a chance to race with the best

equipment of his career, was badly injured.

"I'd rather be anywhere right now but here," said Waltrip, who took the lead 16 laps from the end of the 200-lap race. "The only reason I won this race was Dale Earnhardt."

Waltrip didn't learn until later that Earnhardt had died.

"He wasn't just my owner. He was my friend," Waltrip said. "My heart is hurting."

After Dale Jr. crossed the line 0.124 of a second behind Waltrip, he left his car on pit road and tried to get to the scene of his father's accident.

Although no one will ever know for sure, Earnhardt — known as a relentless and ruthless competitor on the track and a generous, unselfish man off it — died doing something so out of character that it could turn out to be his legacy in the sport he came to define.

Running third on the final lap, with one last chance to perhaps pass Waltrip and his son, Earnhardt chose instead to keep the rest of the field at arm's length, to let his son and the

Waltrip credited his teammate with the victory, saying, "The only reason I won this race was Dale Earnhardt."

newest driver on his team fight it out for the victory while he protected them from the contenders in pursuit. In fact, it appeared as if Earnhardt's focus was not on winning, as it had always been since his rookie season of 1979, but instead simply on preventing the other racers from intruding on "The Earnhardt Connection" 1-2-3 finish.

"It's ironic that people talk about how selfish Dale Earnhardt was on the racetrack. He was a winner and when he buckled that helmet on he was focused on winning. But those of us who knew him off the track know how unselfish he really was," said Dr. Jerry Punch, a TV commentator and close friend of Earnhardt.

That others-first attitude was on display as Earnhardt blocked contenders from advancing on his teammates,

rather than trying to win the race himself.

"The irony is that, for the first time on the track, you saw him be very unselfish in the final laps," Punch said. "In my opinion, he had a car that could have made a move. He could have pulled up in front of Sterling Marlin and maybe Kenny Schrader, probably drafted by and won his second Daytona 500. [Instead], Dale Earnhardt lost his life trying to secure a win for his friend, Michael Waltrip.

"What Dale Earnhardt did in those final laps is what a father would do for a son, who was running right in front of him, or a brother would do for a brother," Punch added. "And Michael Waltrip was like a little brother he never had. [Earnhardt] stayed in the third spot and ran a 180 mph screen. He kept Marlin and Schrader, and the others who didn't have a chance coming down the stretch, behind him so that his son and his friend could have an opportunity to win.

"It was a very unselfish move and one that many of us who have known him for years understood." ➜

No signs of life

The crash began when the back left corner of Earnhardt's famed black No. 3 Chevrolet bumped with Sterling Marlin's Dodge. Earnhardt's car fishtailed slightly and briefly slid to its left, down toward the infield, before suddenly swinging back to the right and cutting across traffic at a sharp angle. His car hit the wall headfirst and Ken Schrader's yellow Pontiac crashed into the passenger side.

With Earnhardt's Chevy already smoking at the front, Schrader's car stayed lodged into its side, forming a T. The cars careened again off the wall, plowing into the final turn and sliding to a stop on the infield grass.

Schrader climbed out of his car and ran to check on Earnhardt. He immediately waved for emergency workers to come help.

"I guess someone got into Dale because Dale got into me and then we went up," said Schrader, who was not injured. "We hit pretty hard, and Dale hit harder."

When emergency workers arrived at the accident scene, Earnhardt was not breathing, had no pulse and had blood in his ears and throat. The first member of the track medical team to reach the car clamped an oxygen mask on Earnhardt and realized he was already too late.

Those close to him, including Dale Earnhardt Jr. (left), were devastated by the loss of a friend and racing legend.

Resuscitation efforts began while he was still in his car, with the first paramedic applying the oxygen mask from the right side window while through the driver's-side window another doctor was administering CPR and a second paramedic held Earnhardt's head. At the same time, firefighters were working to cut the roof off the car to try to facilitate Earnhardt's removal.

"That took about five or 10 minutes, during which time we did CPR," Bohannon said. "When the roof came off, Dr. [Alfred] Alson and I both dentified this was a very bad situation, a 'load-and-go' situation."

Transport to the hospital took less than two minutes, and resuscitation efforts continued during the trip, Bohannon said. A trauma team including a neurosurgeon and several other doctors was waiting when Earnhardt arrived at 4:54 p.m. at the hospital, where he was "placed on a ventilator, multiple IV lines were given, IV fluids, chest tubes, various diagnostic tests," Bohannon said.

"We all did everything we could for him," Bohannon said. "He never showed any signs of life."

Earnhardt was pronounced dead at 5:16 p.m. Eastern Standard Time, 22 minutes after he arrived at the hospital. His wife, Teresa, was at his side. ➜

Costly changes

A dull race the previous year prompted NASCAR to alter the rules and equipment for this Daytona 500. The goal was to slow down the cars and make them run closer together, to produce the kind of tight, thrilling racing that fans love and many drivers hate. Due in large part to those aerodynamic changes, the race produced 49 lead changes among 14 drivers. Last year, there were just nine lead changes and hardly any intense racing.

Insiders said no one was more pleased by the return of old-time racing than Earnhardt, who was considered to be the best and most fearless driver in NASCAR when it came to snaking his way through a pack of speeding cars separated only by inches. No one figured to thrive in such an environment more than Earnhardt.

Instead, Earnhardt's death is the fourth in NASCAR since the start of the 2000 season. Busch Series driver Adam Petty, grandson of seven-time champion Richard Petty, died in May at New Hampshire International Speedway. Winston Cup competitor Kenny Irwin was killed at the same track in July, and Craftsman Truck Series driver Tony Roper died at Texas Motor Speedway in Fort Worth in October.

All three died of the same injury that presumably killed Earnhardt. The fracture is caused when a driver's car decelerates quickly but his head and helmet continue to move forward, causing stress to the neck.

Earnhardt wore an old-fashioned, open-faced helmet and chose not to use some of NASCAR's other basic safety innovations. He refused to wear a Head And Neck Safety (HANS) brace that recently has been touted as a way to help prevent serious head injuries.

Bohannon doubted that a full-face helmet or the HANS device would have saved his life.

"I know the full-face helmet wouldn't have made any difference whatsoever. He had no evidence of facial injuries," Bohannon said. "I don't know if the HANS device would have helped. I suspect not."

Only about one in 10 drivers wore the HANS device Sunday. Those who don't wear it have said it was too uncomfortable and limited their mobility.

"It's difficult to talk about safety devices when we're talking about the loss of someone we cared about so much," Punch said. "The HANS device is a good one. But, even as safe as these cars are, I'm not sure the HANS device would have made

At first look, this 19-car wreck earlier in the race appeared much more horrific.

that much difference with the massive deceleration Dale Earnhardt experienced at 185 mph. Typically in these cases, the driver sustains a fracture to the head. That is not a survivable injury.

"The injuries that are most survivable look the worst," Punch continued. "The violent tumbles dissipate energy slowly and result mostly in broken bones and maybe a concussion. But the ones like Sunday, where the car veers suddenly into the wall, are the worst."

The crash, however, didn't look that serious at first. Most of the fans' attention at the time was on the fight for the checkered flag between Waltrip and Earnhardt Jr. In fact, with two- and three-wide racing and constantly changing positions, there was a far more dangerous-looking wreck 26 laps earlier. The 19-car accident sent Tony Stewart's Pontiac flying through the air and over the roof of another car. Stewart also was taken to the hospital, where he was treated

for a concussion. Earnhardt's crash, meanwhile, was deadly. Two months shy of his 50th birthday, on the final turn of the final lap of his 676th Winston Cup race and his 22nd Daytona 500, The Intimidator lost his life.

And the sport will never be the same without him. ■

King of the Road

IN RACING AND
IN LIFE, NOBODY
DID IT QUITE
LIKE EARNHARDT

**By David Fantle and
Thomas Johnson**

Dale Earnhardt knew the risks. Despite being the first driver killed in the Daytona 500, he was well aware that six of his racing brethren had died of injuries from wrecks in qualifying races for the 500. For all of his 49 years, Earnhardt lived life in the fast lane. The Intimidator, as they called him for his fierce, competitive style, was still at the top of his game, and he bristled when some suggested he permanently park his famous black No. 3 Chevrolet and let the younger guys take over.

For all of his 49 years, Earnhardt lived life in the fast lane.

King of the Road

© WIDE WORLD PHOTO

"If physically and mentally I can't do this, [I'll retire]. If I can't go down in the corner and drive competitively with the next guy and beat him or win a race, that's going to [determine when I stop]," Earnhardt said last year. "Your reflexes and health or whatever is going to tell on you. I don't see it happening in the next three years."

The competitive juices ran in Earnhardt from the start. And he never stopped putting the pedal to the metal. It was high gear or nothing.

A racing family

Dale Earnhardt was born April 29, 1951, in Kannapolis, North Carolina. Although young Earnhardt helped his parents work on the family farm, it was in his pedigree to pursue a career behind the wheel of his race car. Although never a NASCAR Winston Cup series champion, his father, Ralph, was an accomplished driver in his own right. A household name at North Carolina short tracks, the elder

Earnhardt ran up some decent numbers during a 23-year racing career. He won NASCAR's Sportsman Division championship in 1956 and in 1961 posted seven top-10 finishes in eight starts in the Winston Cup series division — good for 17th in the standings. Ralph Earnhardt was inducted in the National Motorsports Press Association's Hall of Fame at Darlington, South Carolina Raceway, as well as the International Motorsports Hall of Fame in Talladega, Alabama.

While Ralph was off racing, Martha Earnhardt, the matriarch of the family, would stay home in Kannapolis and watch over their five children."One time Ralph had went to Daytona one year and I didn't go," she said. "I was home with the kids, Dale, Randy and Danny, and they were just trying my nerves to see how bad they could really upset me. I just grabbed a belt and started swinging, I didn't care who I was going to hit. Dale hollered at Randy

and Danny and said, 'Boys, y'all run. Mom's gone crazy!'"

It was through his father that Earnhardt learned to love and respect the sport of car racing. A high school dropout, Earnhardt began racing Hobby-class cars at local events while still a teenager. He worked full-time during the day, welding and mounting tires, and either racing or tinkering with his cars at night. He used his meager wages to buy parts, sometimes even borrowing money with the hopes of paying back the bank on Monday, after a weekend of racing.

Tragically, his father would never see his son attain international fame. On Sept. 26, 1973, Ralph Earnhardt died of a heart attack at the age of 45, ironically while working on his race car. The tragedy hit Dale Earnhardt hard and gave him a renewed determination to dedicate his life to race-car driving. Earnhardt continued to compete on the Sportsman circuit, racing →

Although never a NASCAR Winston Cup series champion, his father, Ralph, was an accomplished driver in his own right.

With legions of fans everywhere he traveled, Earnhardt was one of most legendary figures in the history of stock-car racing.

King of the Road

Earnhardt made his Winston Cup debut in 1975 in the World 600 at Charlotte Motor Speedway, finishing 22nd in a Dodge owned by Ed Negre, right behind Richard Childress. For his part, Earnhardt earned $2,245. During the next three years, Earnhardt made only eight more starts, ending with the Dixie 500 in Atlanta in 1978. Earnhardt, driving a second car for Rod Osterlund, finished a respectable fourth, one spot behind Osterlund's regular driver Dave Marcis.

This race would prove to be Earnhardt's biggest career break. Marcis left the Osterlund team to form his own. This left an opening and Osterlund, after considering several candidates, tapped Earnhardt to be his driver for the 1979 Winston Cup season. →

at local speedways such as Hickory, Concord and the Metrolina Fairgrounds.

According to Martha Earnhardt, her lifelong exposure to racing through her husband, son and now grandson, is often nerve-racking. "I think it gets worse instead of better," she said. "When you get older, your nerves are not quite as strong.

When Ralph started I was only about 19 years old and I really didn't have sense enough to worry.

"When Dale got in a race car, that was just altogether different from Ralph," she continued. "I grew up with Ralph racing and I knew he knew what he was doing. When Dale got in, that was part of me getting in that car and it was just a different story."

AP/WIDE WORLD PHOTO

Dale Earn

1975 - Made stock-car racing debut on May 25, finishing 22nd in the World 600 at Charlotte Motor Speedway.

1979 - Earned first victory on April 1 at Bristol, Tenn.; Won Rookie of the Year Award.

1980 - Won first Winston Cup Championship, becoming only driver to win Rookie of the Year and season championship back-to-back.

1986 - Won five races to take second Winston Cup Championship.

1987 - Won 11 races for third Winston Cup Championship, finishing in top five 21 times in 29 races.

ardt Career Highlights

1990 - Won nine times to take fourth Winston Cup Championship, earning a then-record $3,083,056.

1991 - Won four races for fifth Winston Cup Championship.

1993 - Won six races to earn sixth Winston Cup Championship.

1994 - Won seventh Winston Cup Championship, tying Richard Petty for most career titles. Topped $3-million mark in earnings for third time in five years.

1996 - Became third driver to start 500 consecutive Winston Cup races.

1997 - Became first driver to reach $30 million in American Motor Sports winnings and first race car driver to appear on box of Wheaties Cereal.

1998 - Won first Daytona 500 in 20th career start, breaking a 59-race winless streak overall. Finished eighth in season standings, his 18th top-10 finish in 20 years.

1999 - Won 10th consecutive Twin 125 qualifying race at Daytona.

2000 - Won Winston 500 on Oct. 15 at Talladega Superspeedway for final career victory.

Career Pole Positions: 22.
Career top 5 finishes: 268.
Career top 10 finishes: 404.

Winston Cup Championships: 7
(1980, 1986, 1987, 1990, 1991, 1993, 1994)

IROC Championships: 3
(1990, 1995, 1999)

American Driver of the Year: 2 (1987, 1994)

Won record nine races at Talladega Superspeedway.

Owns record 34 victories in all forms of racing at Daytona Speedway.

King of the Road

In his inaugural season, Earnhardt took home the rookie title, besting Harry Grant, Terry Labonte and Joe Millikan. This came after Earnhardt scored his first Winston Cup win in just his 16th start, and finished the season with 11 top-five finishes.

Earnhardt continued his impressive record during his sophomore year on the circuit, edging out racing legend Cale Yarborough to win the 1980 NASCAR Winston Cup championship, the first of what would become a regular feat. In the process, Earnhardt became the only driver to win the rookie and championship honors in consecutive years.

Midway through Earnhardt's rookie season, Osterlund sold his team to Jim Stacy. Earnhardt, after competing in just four races, joined forces with Childress, completing the season as a member of his team. Beginning with the 1982 season, Earnhardt competed for Bud Moore and big-buck sponsor Wrangler for two seasons, winning three races and finishing as high as eighth in the overall point standings driving in the number-15 Fords. In an April 1982 race, Earnhardt fractured a knee in a crash at Talladega, but didn't miss a race.

The right stuff

Meanwhile, Childress, with driver Ricky Rudd, was building his team into a powerhouse contender. Earnhardt returned to the Childress team as the 1984 season began. It was a marriage made in racing heaven. After just two years of competition, Earnhardt won the 1986 Winston Cup championship.

In 1986, Earnhardt began cementing his legendary status on the racetrack, collecting six more Winston Cup championships over a nine-season period, tying Richard Petty for the most championships (seven) in a single career. Together, Earnhardt and Childress won championships in 1986, '87, '90, '91, '93 and '94. He finished second in the standings to Bobby Labonte last year and was determined to make a run for a record eighth championship in the 2001 season.

In 1990, Earnhardt earned a then-record $3 million in prize money. His career winnings exceeded $41 million.

Daytona at last

In February 1998, Earnhardt was named to the list of NASCAR's 50 greatest drivers as the sport marked its 50th anniversary, joining his late father on that list. That same year he finally won the Daytona 500, setting off a memorable celebration that included him spinning his car across the grass in the track's trioval.

While it seemed that Earnhardt had racked up wins in every major NASCAR racing event, one title that had eluded him was the Daytona 500. In what would be the capping of an illustrious career, Earnhardt won the 1998 race, the 71st win of his career in 575 races. This would come after his 20th attempt at Daytona. ➜

In 1990, Earnhardt earned a then-record $3 million in prize money. His career winnings exceeded $41 million.

Earnhardt hoists his trophy after winning the 1990 Checker 500 at Phoenix International Raceway.

King of the Road

The long-awaited victory was emotional and sweet for Earnhardt. "Yes! Yes! Yes!," he exalted after the win. "Twenty years! Can you believe it!"

Although he won the Daytona 500 only once (1998), Earnhardt was Daytona's all-time leader with 34 victories at the storied track. About his 500 win, Earnhardt said: "This win is for all of our fans and all the people who told me, 'Dale, this is your year.' There was a lot of hard work that went into this and I have to thank every member of the Richard Childress Racing team. I have had a lot of great fans and people behind me all through the years and I just can't thank them enough ... The Daytona 500 is over. And we won it! We won it!"

After the Daytona win, the most popular and charismatic figure in stock-car racing history went on the talk-show circuit, even appearing on "Late Night With David Letterman." There he good-naturedly read "Dale Earnhardt's Top 10 Reasons It Took Me 20 Years To Win The Daytona 500." Among the reasons:

- It took me 19 years to realize I had the emergency brake on.
- Finally rotated and balanced my mustache. ➜

Earnhardt embraces daughter Nicole at the 1991 Busch Clash.

On top of his game to the bitter end

The common sense in all of us tries to tell us that Dale Earnhardt Sr. never should have gone down this way, with his car becoming his coffin on the last lap of the Daytona 500.

The sensible side says that a 49-year old man should've given up his seat in the cockpit of a race car going nearly 200 miles per hour. Or at least he should've announced his retirement, backed off the pedal and rode around on a nice farewell tour.

Earnhardt, however, was not a common driver, and the words 'back off' did not evolve in his vocabulary. He had no reason to back off. Age should not be the maxim by which retirement is measured. Ability should be that yardstick, and if we're measuring it that way then Earnhardt was nowhere near the rocking chair.

He had ability and he had a goal: to win his eighth Winston Cup championship and break the tie of seven titles he shared with fellow NASCAR legend Richard Petty.

Earnhardt's driving skills had not eroded anywhere close to the point that he was a detriment to other drivers. He was a detriment to the other drivers because he could still outrun them, still battle them side-by-side through a turn and still plant them into a wall if he deemed it appropriate.

Earnhardt still had plenty left, evidenced by last year's second-place finish in the NASCAR Winston Cup standings. You don't put a thoroughbred out to pasture in his prime, and you don't take away a driver's wheel when he's still capable of winning.

In fact, Earnhardt was still so good and so tough that it made his death in a racing crash almost inconceivable.

The common-sense side of us wishes Earnhardt had walked away a little sooner and lived to watch his son become a Winston Cup champion. But Earnhardt was an uncommon driver and an uncommon competitor. You can't ask someone of that caliber to walk away at the top of his craft. Earnhardt might never have walked away, so perhaps he went down in the most appropriate way possible. He was in a race car, unselfishly paving the way for his son to possibly win the Daytona 500, and because of that he died with uncommon valor.

That is how most drivers would like to be remembered, and how most will remember Earnhardt.

"I've told my wife many times, 'If anything ever happens to me in a race car, you just remember it was exactly what I was wanting to do,' " said Winston Cup veteran Mike Wallace. "The only thing I can say is it's what Dale Earnhardt wanted to do. He died doing what he loved to do."

How many of us in life get to go out that way?

– By Jeff Bartlett, NASCAR writer for Checkered Flag magazine.

Dale Earnhardt Tribute   **23**

King of the Road

- My new pit crew — The Spice Girls.
- This year, whenever I'd pass somebody, I'd give 'em the finger.

The legend grows

After the Daytona win, Earnhardt's legend grew, and so did the demand for his services.

In May 1998, Earnhardt made a guest voice appearance as himself on the animated FOX series, "King of the Hill."

"I had a great time working with the people from 'King of the Hill,'" Earnhardt said. "It was a surprise when they asked if I was interested in doing a part for the show. After talking to the writers I found out they are big NASCAR fans and they followed the series."

That same year he made a cameo appearance in the feature film *BASEketball*. In his screen debut, Earnhardt played a washed-up racecar driver who drives a taxi cab for a living.

"It was fun," Earnhardt said of his acting stint. "When we first arrived on the set, the crew stopped what they were doing and started applauding and congratulating me on the win. I guess they all got together on Sunday and watched the race. It was very flattering."

A beaming mother, Martha Earnhardt said, "I'm proud Dale has got to do what he has always wanted to do, and has really done well at it. He has been able to come as far and accomplish what he has, and I am just proud of him as a person, the person he has become.

"It's really amazing when you go to the grocery store and there's your kid's picture on a cereal box or a Sun-drop bottle, or you see him on a billboard on the side of the road. It's really hard to realize that's really your child."

Sixth on NASCAR's all-time win list with 76 victories, Earnhardt was enjoying a late-career resurgence. He finished second in the 2000

points standings to Bobby Labonte, a remarkable feat at his age.

In 1999, Earnhardt underwent back surgery for what doctors called an "anterior cervical discectomy and fusion (or ruptured disc in his spinal column)." The operation was considered a success and Earnhardt stayed out of his car for about six weeks, the longest absence of his storied career.

After the surgery Earnhardt returned with a vengeance in 2000. With a diversified business portfolio that included ownership of three Winston Cup teams for son Dale Earnhardt Jr., Steve Park and Michael Waltrip, as well as part-time operation for oldest son Kerry Earnhardt, his desire to get behind the wheel and compete never waned.

The year 2000 saw the 49-year-old racer again in the thick of the hunt for his eighth Winston Cup championship. Earnhardt's final career victory came on October 15 of last season at Talladega, Alabama, on the day Tony Roper ➜

Sixth on NASCAR's all-time win list with 76 victories, Earnhardt was enjoying a late-career resurgence.

All was well after this triumph at the 1995 Brickyard 400.

King of the Road

died from injuries he'd suffered in a Truck series crash at Texas Motor Speedway the night before.

It was a turnaround year for Earnhardt who was almost written off after going winless in 1997. The 1998 Daytona 500 win was to be his only victory that season. Still the veteran racer would hear nothing of retirement.

"I've got four years of racing left, at least," he said last summer. "Who knows? I might even drive another car with my own team. I'm not ruling anything out. I've got a job and an opportunity to win that eighth championship. That's what we're focusing on. That's what we're driving for. That's what we're working for.

"We're doing it with a more solid team than I've had in past years," he added. "I may have been hurt for the last two years and working with pain and stuff and didn't realize it until it got worse and worse. I had to have something to do about it. That's all in the past. It's over. We're healthy. The team is healthy."

Hands-on

Because of his tenacity and fierce competitive nature, Earnhardt was considered by race fans as either the most hated or most loved driver in NASCAR. About his manic schedule, fellow racing Hall-of-Famer Buddy Baker said jokingly, "I guess that's the price you pay to make $40 million."

For his part, Earnhardt fessed up to his workaholic tendencies. "I'm the kind of guy, I want to know everything," he said. "I want to know if there's an unhappy employee somewhere. I want to know what the balance is at the end of the day. If I know what's going on, then I can help in some way or control it."

Earnhardt's wife, Teresa, is also heavily involved in the business, handling several duties for the 300-employee corporation. The company is located on 350 acres of rolling farmland in the north Charlotte suburbs. It's housed in four buildings occupying more than 200,000 square feet, including the 108,000 square-foot main building.

Late last year, Earnhardt became part owner of a baseball team in the South Atlantic League, the Piedmont Boll Weevils, who changed their affiliation to the Chicago White Sox for this season. The franchise also changed its name to the driver's nickname, becoming the Kannapolis Intimidators.

But Earnhardt was more than just the weathered-looking and imposing mustachioed man behind the dark glasses. Said *The Charlotte Observer*: "He was a businessman who owned race teams and chicken farms. He was a genius for marketing his 'Intimidator' image, which sold a lot of T-shirts while also allowing him to carve out at least a small piece of privacy for him and his family." ➜

Earnhardt was considered by race fans as either the most hated or most loved driver in NASCAR.

King of the Road

Earnhardt's popularity was chiefly responsible for enabling the sport's evolution from a regional pastime in the Southeast to a billion-dollar industry on the national stage. In fact, FOX only recently began airing NASCAR events to high viewership ratings. Fox's coverage of the 2001 Daytona 500 race earned an 8.4 rating and 19 share, the highest overnight rating for the race since 1986.

Stock-car racing has been rapidly growing in popularity, and Earnhardt is largely responsible. "Nobody has had more to do with that than No. 3," said *The Charlotte Observor.* "Dale Earnhardt was the embodiment of stock-car racing. He was its most honest image. He was dark speed, an Elvis smile, a blithe spirit who knew that racing was just that, racing, and really all the rules you needed were to race like a man and keep the pedal on the floor."

"Dale Earnhardt was the greatest race-car driver that ever lived," Ned Jarrett, a former NASCAR champion himself, told the Associated Press. "He could do things with a race car that no one else could."

The Intimidator to the end

As recently as last year, Earnhardt spoke about the sport that he loved as if he was just beginning his legendary career. "I'd like to win 25 more races before I quit racing," he said, "and I'd like to win another championship. That's on my list of things to do."

A racing purist, Earnhardt at times was critical of NASCAR for rules that he said were designed to slow drivers down. He preferred the 1980s when he and fellow drivers Darrell Waltrip and Rusty Wallace did a lot of "gouging and sticking." Today's racers, said Earnhardt, ride in a pack — "existing on the track together" — waiting for the perfect moment to

make the one move that could win the race. Ironically, at the 2001 Daytona 500, it was Earnhardt who may have exacted those rules in order to preserve the victory during the final lap of the race won by Michael Waltrip, driving a car Earnhardt owned.

"It's like having the privilege to race to win," Earnhardt said. "Guys play in the minor leagues and never get to go to the majors. Guys get to race in Busch or the truck series and never get an opportunity to drive a Cup car. I'm there. I have the opportunity. I'm excited about what I do. I'm not content with not winning. If somebody tells you I'm riding my years out, they're not paying attention."

The racing world never stopped paying attention to Dale Earnhardt. In addition to his mother, Martha, Earnhardt is survived by his wife, Teresa; two sons, Dale Jr., 27 and Kerry, 32, and two daughters, Kelly, 29 and Taylor Nicole, 13. ∎

As recently as last year, Earnhardt spoke about the sport that he loved as if he was just beginning his legendary career.

The Intimi

dator

AP/WIDE WORLD PHOTOS

THE ONE-
OF-A-KIND
EARNHARDT
MORE THAN
LIVED UP TO
HIS NICKNAME

By James Raia

More than flat tires, oil leaks or blown transmissions, Dale Earnhardt gave his fellow NASCAR drivers their biggest concern — intimidation.

"There is no worse sight than seeing Dale Earnhardt in your rear-view mirror with one lap left," was the refrain repeated for more than two decades by veteran and rookie drivers alike.

It helped Earnhardt earn the nickname of "The Intimidator," a moniker that defined the driver's aggressive and fearless racing style throughout his 76 career wins and 676 career Winston Cup events.

When he crashed and died in the final yards of the 2001 Daytona 500, Earnhardt was competing in his 648th consecutive event — seven starts shy of Terry Labonte's record. His car was recorded with a 12th-place finish, a fatal, eerie start and end to what Earnhardt had hoped would lead to a record-setting eighth season championship. ➜

Old habits die hard

There wasn't much of a clue of Earnhardt's future racing prowess when he made his NASCAR debut in May 1975 in the World 600 at Charlotte Motor Speedway. He started in 33rd position and finished 22nd, some 45 laps behind winner Richard Petty.

But in April 1979 at Bristol, Tennessee, Earnhardt's cavalcade of career victories began. And so did his legacy as a tough-as-nails competitor.

Skilled, brash and savvy, he tried maneuvering into openings on race tracks observers said other drivers couldn't even see. And just like country singer Johnny Cash, Earnhardt's image was enhanced by his trademark black attire and strong opinions. In addition to "The Intimidator," others called him "Ironhead" or "The Man in Black."

Regardless of what he was called, Earnhardt was a man of hard-to-break traditions. He proudly wore his black jeans, black shirt and trademark thick mustache. He also preferred to wear an open-face helmet while driving. Many of his colleagues had switched to the more safety-conscious, full-face helmets, but Earnhardt said he could see better in the traditional helmet.

He drove a black race car, No. 3. The combined color and number became so popular, race fans simply put black "3" decals on their cars. Words weren't required.

Even *The Charlotte Observer* editorial cartoonist used the black 3 to honor Earnhardt. In the edition printed the day following the driver's death, the newspaper ran a three-panel cartoon. The first panel was a black 3, the second a 3 sprouting racing wings and in the third, the 3 had transformed into just the race wings.

Whether using his icy stare or rough tactics, Earnhardt was the master of intimidation.

Again, words weren't necessary.

In the 21-year span of racing since he claimed his first title until his final win on October 15 last year at Talladega, Alabama, Earnhardt won at least one race in 19 seasons. He won two races or more in 15 seasons, including the first of his seven Winston Cup titles in 1980 when he claimed five races.

Earnhardt won 11 times in 29 starts in 1987 and nine times in 29 starts in 1990. He compiled 281 top-five and 428 top-10 finishes in his career. Last season, he competed in 35 events, the most season starts in his career. With the half-century age

plateau approaching, Earnhardt still won twice.

In recent years, when NASCAR safety innovations were introduced, Earnhardt dismissed them, including his refusal to wear the HANS (Head And Neck Safety) brace recently introduced as a way to help prevent serious head injuries. Earnhardt also preferred to use a low-back seat, long after competitors had switched to high-back seats.

When restrictor carburetor plates were ordered by NASCAR last season to slow speed and hopefully have drivers run closer together, Earnhardt bawked. "A race driver hates a

restrictor plate," he said. "I think the same thing I've always thought about restrictor plates. It's not racing. Racing is going out there and trying to be the fastest guy on the track."

Earnhardt followed the racing roots of his father Ralph, a well-known competitor at short-track circuits throughout the Carolinas. As a boy, he watched his father build engines and cars. And when his father died of a heart attack when Earnhardt was in his 20s, he knew what his future held. "When he passed away, Earnhardt explained in a 1999 interview with *The Washington Post*, "I felt like, 'I have to do this. I've got to do this.' " ➜

Earnhardt shunned some of the safety features utilized by his peers, such as the HANS (Head And Neck Safety) brace.

Building a reputation

After four years of only a combined handful of Winston Cup races, Earnhardt got his first victory in 1979 in his first full season. The win propelled him to Winston Cup rookie of the year honors. He followed in 1980 with his initial season championship.

Through the 1980s, Earnhardt's driving style continued to give further credence to his moniker. Fellow drivers and race fans knew Earnhardt as gruff, stubborn and arrogant — all traits that suited his aggressive racing ways and made him his sport's most controversial and respected driver.

Earnhardt was perhaps best known for maneuvering his way through tight packs of cars that were often separated by inches. Some drivers said he was so skilled at drafting — the process of using the slipstream of an opponent's car to your own advantage — that friend and fellow-champion Dale Jarrett once said he believed Earnhardt could "see the air."

Earnhardt also had his detractors. He was often booed as much as he was cheered by some fans. There were many race followers who felt Earnhardt was a bully and drove to his wins by risking his own safety and the safety of others by purposely knocking others out of races. Still, none of his competitors questioned Earnhardt's skills.

"NASCAR lost its greatest driver and probably the greatest driver it will ever have," said fellow competitor Johnny Benson. "Our sport will go on, but I don't think it will ever be the same."

Beyond his uncanny ability to get to the front of the pack, it was his wont to remain there that highlighted much of Earnhardt's career.

During the 1980s, it seemed nearly every week he was involved ➜

The Intimidator waged some of his fiercest battles with Gordon and his colorful DuPont-sponsored car.

Though an intimidator behind the wheel, Earnhardt was gracious to his many supporters.

in fender-bumping battles with his top competitors, not the least of whom were Geoff Bodine, Darrell Waltrip and Bill Elliott.

Among fans and his peers, Earnhardt had a reputation as a driver who would take chances others wouldn't. At the Atlanta Motor Speedway, for instance, he would pass drivers using an outside groove, an almost unheard-of strategy.

In 1992, at the International Race of Champions (IROC) in Charlotte, he somehow shot from third to win the race in the final few hundred yards. The following year, he won four consecutive Winston Cup races, becoming the third modern-era driver to win four straight events.

Another example of Earnhardt's brash racing approach occurred in 1995 at Bristol Motor Speedway. Early in a race on the high-banked, half-mile oval, NASCAR officials relegated Earnhardt to the back of the field for knocking Rusty Wallace into a wall. Earnhardt had also collided with Derrick Cope and Lake Speed, leaving his car badly battered.

Despite his car's demolition-derby appearance, Earnhardt was in second place on the final turn. He rammed into race leader and eventual winner Labonte as the duo approached the finish line. Earnhardt didn't win, but he ended the day in defiance, forcing Labonte to spin awkwardly as he crossed the finish line.

Even when it appeared he had crashed out of events, he sometimes refused to quit. In his well-documented ambulance escape, Earnhardt finished the 1997 Daytona 500 after being taken to an ambulance after his car had flipped in the backstretch of the speedway.

Frustrated by the circumstances of the day, Earnhardt walked out of the ambulance, returned to his tattered car and drove it across the finish line.

Even in his final NASCAR win last October at Talladega, Earnhardt was victorious in grand fashion. The day after Tony Roper died from injuries suffered in a Truck series crash at Texas Motor Speedway, Earnhardt was in 18th place in the waning laps.

The race was the first in which NASCAR used a new set of aerodynamic rules, established to reduce space. Despite his disdain for the new rules, Earnhardt got to the front and earned his 76th career title. The win gave him the sixth-most career titles in race history, the most for an active driver.

"Dale Earnhardt was the greatest driver who ever lived — he could do things with a car no one else could," said former NASCAR champion Ned Jarrett, the father of Dale Jarrett. "He leaves a big, big void here that will be very hard to fill."

To the very end

Even during the final two races of his life, Earnhardt demonstrated his unique racing style. In the IROC race and Daytona 500 preamble, Eddie Cheever and Earnhardt bumped, with Earnhardt falling out of contention. But when the race was over, Earnhardt drove up behind Cheever, spun him out of control and the two drivers exchanged words.

Cheever was apologetic after the race, commenting, "The last thing I need is a feud with Dale Earnhardt."

In his fatal Daytona 500 finale, Earnhardt bumped Sterling Marlin to go into the lead on the 40th lap. He and friend Jeff Gordon "traded paint" at one point during the race. And then there were several instances when The Intimidator nudged rookies Ron Hornaday and Kurt Busch. In Busch's instance, Earnhardt, frustrated by his inability to pass the young and slow driver, finally made his move. While he sped away, Earnhardt made an obscene gesture out of the window.

Earnhardt, who led the race four times for a total of 17 laps, made one pass by maneuvering his car down to the bottom of the concrete oval where he saw an apparent opening. As two wheels slipped into the infield grass, track radio announcer Eli Gould shouted, "The grass is just green asphalt to Earnhardt."

On the final stretch, many observers felt Earnhardt slowed down to fend off others from possibly defeating Michael Waltrip, whom he thought of as a younger brother, and his son, Dale Earnhardt, Jr.

Such was Earnhardt's legacy. When details of the crash that took his life began to unfold, fellow racers couldn't believe The Intimidator wouldn't race again. "After the race was over, I heard things didn't look very good, but, man, Earnhardt?" driver Jeremy Mayfield said. "You figure he'll bounce right back."

A few hours after Earnhardt's death, fans began arriving to mourn at Earnhardt race shops and family residences in North Carolina. Flags were hung at half-staff in several locations. Burning candles and flowers were positioned around photographs of the deceased driver as tributes.

And there were several handmade signs, one of which perhaps best addressed the loss of Dale Earnhardt.

"It's hard to lose a hero, but at least we've got the memories," the sign read. "RIP, Intimidator." ∎

Bumping and nudging opponents was business as usual for the No. 3 Chevy, which spent plenty of time in the repair garage.

Bittersweet
Memories

FOR EARNHARDT, DAYTONA WAS A PLACE OF TRIUMPH, FRUSTRATION AND, ULTIMATELY, TRAGEDY

By James Raia

During his legendary career, Dale Earnhardt competed on famed race tracks and on circuits he would have likely just as soon forgotten. But the Daytona International Speedway was his favorite and most successful venue. In a career that spanned five decades, Earnhardt won 32 races at the track — nearly half of his career victories — and more than any other NASCAR driver. Through bad luck and various other twists of fate, Daytona was both Earnhardt's hell and his most cherished place away from his North Carolina home.

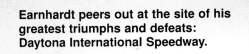

Earnhardt peers out at the site of his
greatest triumphs and defeats:
Daytona International Speedway.

Bittersweet Memories

Despite victories in other events at the speedway and four second-place finishes in the last eight years at the Daytona 500, it took Earnhardt 20 attempts until he captured the event he longed to win throughout his career. Earnhardt claimed the 1998 Daytona 500, his only victory of that season in 33 races. But it was a race that capsulized a career that emerged from boyhood memories of watching his father race to Earnhardt's emergence as an elder statesman of the NASCAR circuit.

Earnhardt sometimes was a man of few words, sometimes not. He was both after winning the Daytona 500. "Yes!, Yes!, Yes!,"

he exclaimed as he popped his head out of the No. 3 Chevrolet on Victory Lane. Earnhardt's victory was claimed at an average speed of 172.712 mph, the third-fastest in the race's history. It also occurred as if planned with perfect timing for NASCAR's 50th anniversary season. The win also allowed Earnhardt to earn a record $1,059,015 and end his nearly two-year winless streak of 59 races. "Everybody over the last week has said, 'This is your year,' " Earnhardt said in the next day's edition of *The Charlotte Observer*. "Man, they were so adamant about it. They knew something I didn't, I reckon."

Although he had already won 70 races in his career, the Daytona 500 title had eluded him for so long, his emotions could finally be displayed — sort of. "I cried a little bit in the race car on the way to the checkered flag," Earnhardt said. "Well, maybe not cried, but at least my eyes watered up."

A memorable day

Unlike many of his disappointing last-lap finishes at Daytona, Earnhardt's historic win was not anti-climactic, but it was void of any last-second heroics or the frustrations that often marked his career. Earnhardt took the lead on the 140th of the 200-lap race when he passed teammate Mike Skinner on Turn 4. He retained the lead when he pitted for fuel and right-side tires with less than 27 laps to go.

"We just kept playing our cards," Earnhardt recalled. "The others would go this way or that way and I would go with them. What I was hoping for was that they'd stay close in line and when it got down to five [laps] to go, they would start racing behind me. That made me feel better because I could pick who I wanted to dice with."

Racing under ever-darkening skies, a threat of rain and Earnhardt's long history of late-race mishaps, added to the drama. But the luck of the day finally went Earnhardt's way. "When we came out in front on that pit stop, I just knew that Dale Earnhardt was going to lead the race the rest of the way," said Richard Childress, the car owner.

With one lap left, the Ford driven by ➜

The Intimidator became the celebrator after claiming the long-awaited Daytona 500 victory.

Bittersweet
Memories

Jimmy Spencer collided into John Andretti's Pontiac. Andretti's car spun, knocking into Lake Speed's Ford. The crash brought out the third caution of the day. As a result, Earnhardt, who led the race five times for a total of 105 laps, won ironically under a caution flag.

A record crowd of 185,000 witnessed the highly emotional race on the famous high-banked trioval track. Even the crews and representatives of other teams stood in unison and cheered as Earnhardt ended his one racing stigma. Well-wishers in the pit row rushed out to congratulate the long overdue winner. There were smiles and laughter and tears of joy. Earnhardt then drove his car into the field and did two "doughnuts" before pulling into Victory Lane for a long celebration.

"It was my time," Earnhardt said. "I have been passed on the last lap, I have run out of gas and I have had a cut tire. I don't care how we won it, but that we won it.

"It's a feeling you can't replace," he continued. "It's eluded us for so many years. The drama and excitement of it all has built so much over the years. There have been a lot of emotions played out down here at Daytona with the letdowns we've had."

A relationship begins

Three years after he began his NASCAR career, Earnhardt first raced at Daytona on July 4, 1978. He finished seventh in the Pepsi 400 while driving a Ford. But while there were many victories and many other tracks, Earnhardt's affinity for Daytona's 2.5-mile super speedway and its 31-degree bank track rapidly grew as his career progressed.

Since 1989, Earnhardt had claimed at least one race every year at Daytona. And even in the final races of his career, three months shy of age 50, he wanted more wins. In the International Race of Champions (IROC) two days prior to the 2001 Daytona 500, Earnhardt was racing for the lead. But Eddie Cheever ran him into the grass on the first turn and catapulted Dale Jarrett to the win.

Although Earnhardt and Cheever exchanged words, The Intimidator remained unscathed. "I've got one shot left," Earnhardt said, in an eerie reference to the pending final race of his life. "Maybe it's a good omen for the 500."

As it turned out, the omen was anything but good. When Earnhardt crashed and was killed in the waning seconds of the 2001 Daytona 500, it marked the end of the most unique relationship between a driver and a race track in racing history. "NASCAR has lost its greatest driver, ever," said Bill France Jr., the circuit's chairman.

But the track in which he lost his life was also the track of his greatest success and ➜

Jubilant triumphs and bitter disappointments were par for the course at Daytona.

Bittersweet Memories

AP/WIDE WORLD PHOTO

frustrations. It was also the venue in which he earned a good percentage of his record career earnings of $41,640,462.

Earnhardt's legacy and his death brought out emotional comments from the racing world. But many of his associates had similarly admiring and respectful thoughts.

They were all perhaps summed succinctly by Dan Davis of Ford Racing. "Dale Earnhardt transcended NASCAR," Davis said.

It may have taken Earnhardt 20 attempts to win the race he coveted the most, but there were plenty of other crowns on the Daytona circuit. He won the Pepsi 400 twice and also captured seven Busch Grand Nationals titles, seven Goody's 300s, 12 Twin 125 events, including 10 straight from 1990-1999; six Budweiser Shootouts and six IROC titles. Earnhardt particularly enjoyed the IROC races, since it gave him the opportunity to showcase his driving talents to drivers from other racing circuits.

But for as many wins as he accumulated despite a career replete with injuries, there were nearly as many disappointments. The Daytona 500 win made up for the other disappointments, but it may have been Earnhardt's losses that helped build his legacy as much as his career of dominance.

In the 1986 Daytona 500, he ran out of tricks, allowing Geoff Bodine to win. In 1990, Earnhardt led for most the race. But he suffered a cut tire that sprung rookie Derrike Cope the crown.

The following year, Earnhardt could have been on his way to victory again when an accident with the late Davey Allison pushed Ernie Irvan to the win. In two more instances, Earnhardt finished second by a combined

AP/WIDE WORLD PHOTO

time of .73 seconds. In 1995, he was the runner-up to Sterling Marlin by .61 seconds.

The following year, his margin of loss was only .12 seconds to Dale Jarrett. "Racing someone and running second hasn't been too bad," said Earnhardt. "Letdowns of being dominant and not winning really worked on Richard and me. To come out here and race in a competitive race and not be that dominant, but still be dominant enough to lead most of the race and win, makes you feel proud of what you've accomplished with your team. We worked hard to win the Daytona 500."

That is what Dale Earnhardt always did. He worked hard, always with two things in mind: driving fast and winning. ■

Continui a Lega

EARNHARDT JR. WILL STRIVE TO
UPHOLD HIS FAMILY'S TRADITION

By Jason Wilde

It was only a dream. It came to Dale Earnhardt Jr. last month, a few weeks before he was to race in his second Daytona 500, the same race that it took his legendary father, Dale Earnhardt Sr., 20 years to win.

"I'm pretty confident that I'm going to win the Daytona 500. Because I've dreamed about it so much," he said. "You can call me crazy, but I'll be talking to you at the post-race interview, talking about how I did it."

In the dream, he did it the easy way. "Out front all day," he said. "It was so real, it was crazy."

And where was his legendary father? "He wasn't there," Earnhardt Jr. said.

Sadly, tragically, when Earnhardt Jr. crossed the finish line in the 2001 Daytona 500 — second, 0.124 of a second behind teammate Michael Waltrip — his father was not there. Dale Sr.'s familiar black No. 3 Chevrolet had crashed seconds before the checkered

flag, less than half a mile from the finish line, into the concrete outside retaining wall in Turn 4 of Daytona International Speedway. He died instantly.

Suddenly, Earnhardt Jr. had lost the man who meant everything to him. Instead of celebrating Dale Earnhardt Inc.'s 1-2 finish, Dale Jr. crossed the finish line, parked his car at pit row and immediately tried to get to the scene of the crash he'd seen in his rearview mirror. And this was no dream.

Last season, Dale Jr. wrote a story about his father that he planned to post on NASCAR's official web site. Before he sent it in, though, he wanted to read it to his father. So one day after a meeting in his dad's office, he stayed behind. As soon as the doors were shut, he started reading the story, part of which reads, "This man [Dale Sr.] could lead the world's finest army. He has wisdom that knows no bounds. No fire could burn his character, no stone could break it. Every ➜

Continuing a Legacy

step he takes has purpose. Every walk has reason."

"That was something special," Earnhardt Sr. told *Sports Illustrated* last December. "You know, he tells me he loves me all the time, but when you hear something like that, well, it really gets you. Racing, and just being around each other more, has brought us closer."

And now, just like that, the father is gone. And the son must somehow find the strength to go on racing without him. It won't be easy.

A victory in the 500 would have helped Earnhardt Jr. forget the disappointment of the second half of his rookie season. Earnhardt Jr. joined his father in the Winston Cup Series last year, won two races plus the non-points Winston race — NASCAR's version of an all-star game — in the season's first half. But Earnhardt Jr. did not have a top-10 finish in the last 21 races. He wound up 16th in the points standings.

"There were a lot of things. We had a lot of problems. We all had ego problems, we all had personality problems," Earnhardt Jr. said of himself and his team. "We just all lost respect for each other, me and my teammates, and me and my crew. We just kind of let it go to our heads, the success we had at the first half of the year. And we couldn't repeat that like we wanted to. We never really pointed fingers at each other, but we did let each other know we weren't happy."

But this was the start of a new season, a new year. Everything was going to be different. And now, just one race into the season, he must go on with a heavy heart. He'd lost more than just a race. He'd lost the owner of his team, the man who raised him in the sport. He'd lost his father.

Dale Jr., 26, is the second child from his father's second marriage and the third of Dale Sr.'s four children. Dale Jr.'s sister, Kelly, is two years older. Dale Jr.'s older half-brother — Kerry, the oldest, from Dale's first marriage — also races occasionally on the Busch circuit. They also have a younger half-sister, Taylor, from Dale's third marriage to Teresa, who was at Dale Sr.'s bedside when he was pronounced dead.

"I never thought Dale Jr. was going to be a driver," Dale Sr. said. "He never seemed to have the interest. He wasn't one of those kids who always wanted to be around the garage, to see how things worked. What's happened has kind of surprised me."

"I always wanted to be a driver," Dale Jr. countered. "There always was this idea, though, that you had to sweep the floor for a year before you ever got a chance to touch a wrench. I didn't want to sweep the floor." ➜

Earnhardt Jr. finished in second place, only 0.124 of a second behind Waltrip at this year's Daytona 500.

Continuing a Legacy

Asked during his Winston Cup rookie year about working for his dad, Dale Jr. replied: "Just like every other boss. He ain't no super jerk or nothin'. Actually, having him for a father is pretty cool, because of what he knows, because of everything he's done and his experience."

But being close to his father had been a challenge throughout Dale Jr.'s life. Until he was 6, Dale Jr. and Kelly lived with their mother. When they moved into their father's house in 1980, Dale Sr. was winning his first Winston Cup championship, in his second year on the circuit. And as NASCAR grew in popularity and his father's schedule grew more hectic, time with Dad was in even shorter supply.

And when they did manage to get together, it was hard. "I always wanted Dale Jr. to get an education," Dale Sr. said. "I always talked about that. My biggest regret is that I dropped out of school in ninth grade. My father told me it was a mistake. I just wouldn't listen. I wanted to make sure Dale Jr. didn't make the same mistake. It was a battle, but we got him through."

"Education was such a big thing. So I graduated from high school, and where was my father? He didn't come to graduation. He was in a race somewhere," Dale Jr. said. "I understand now, of course, but I was looking forward to holding that diploma in his face. Except he wasn't there. He was at some other end of the earth."

Dale Sr. had also grown up in a racing family, but that was long before the sport had taken off. Back then,

A victory at Daytona would have eased the pain of a difficult second half of Dale Jr.'s rookie season.

when his father, Ralph Earnhardt, won the 1956 NASCAR Sportsman championship, the races were usually on Saturday nights in North Carolina and Georgia. After Ralph's races, the family would drive home together and have a party. There wasn't the father-son separation that there was when Dale Jr. was growing up.

But racing finally brought father and son together. As a kid, Dale Jr. would go to the go-kart track, where his father would stand a few feet from the wall, making him drive through a narrow space in between. With each lap, Dale Sr. would stand a little closer to the wall, to teach his son how to take the best angle on the turns. Dale Jr. became serious about racing in 1991, his senior year of high school, and Dad would bring Dale Jr. through the short-track ranks and into the Busch

Series full-time in 1998, when he won the first of two championships.

"I'm going through a lot of the things my father's been through, and I'm starting to understand him more," Dale Jr. said earlier this year. "I feel we're able to relate to each other easier."

But that's not to say that being on the same track together week-in and week-out hasn't resulted in the two having their rough moments. Like last year during Dale Jr.'s first Daytona 500, when he ended up 13th and his father finished 21st.

The two raced with each other — or within a few positions of each other — during much of the second half of the race, pushing their way into the top five at times with the son racing behind his dad. But as the end neared, Earnhardt Jr. got antsy. He left his father behind, opting to work with other drivers while his father struggled. Earnhardt Jr. passed his father on lap 177 of the 200-lap race with the help of race-winner Dale Jarrett.

"When me and dad were hooked up in the draft, we really couldn't get anybody to stay behind us and couldn't get anybody to work with us," ➔

Continuing a **Legacy**

Earnhardt Jr. said afterward. "So that's when I thought, 'Get out of the way! Get out of the way!' I just wanted everybody to get out of the way. I was willing to hook up [and draft] with anybody."

"I thought he would be the first one to help me, but he was the last person who wanted to stay behind me. We did more racing than I wanted to. I wanted to stay with him and stay behind him. Then, everybody got to racing behind me and it was either pass or be passed."

Had father and son worked together, it could have been a family affair in Victory Lane. Earnhardt had moved to fourth and Little E to fifth, right on his father's bumper, and the two swapped positions, sparring back and forth before the son struck out on his own. His father reacted angrily.

"He didn't work at all with anybody," Earnhardt said of his son. "He wanted to pass. That's all he wanted to do, so that's why he finished where he did."

Even less than a week before Dale Sr.'s death, father and son had an on-track run-in. In a group of cars battling for the lead with three laps remaining in the Budweiser Shootout, Earnhardt Jr. lost inside position to his father and Rusty Wallace. Earnhardt Jr. dropped from second to sixth, losing any chance at victory.

"I helped [my dad] out a few times, and he got me in the lead a few times.

But when it comes down to the last 10 laps, ain't nobody going to be helping you," Earnhardt Jr. said. Asked about his dad's late-race maneuver, Dale Jr. replied diplomatically, "I was surprised."

But there were some great father-and-son moments, too. For his second Winston Cup victory last May, Earnhardt Jr. passed his father with 31 laps to go in the Pontiac Excitement 400 and held on to become the first repeat winner of the season.

Last August, Dale Sr., Dale Jr. and Kerry all ran in the Pepsi 400, just the second race in NASCAR Winston Cup history where a father raced against two sons. Dad finished sixth, while Dale Jr., who started on the pole, finished 31st. Kerry, making his Cup debut, finished last after crashing on lap 6.

And last Father's Day weekend in Long Pond, Pa., Kerry won the Pocono ARCA 200 for the first victory of his career — with his dad on the radio, talking him through it — while Sr. and Jr. started side-by-side on the eighth row at the Pocono 500.

And earlier this month, Dale Sr. and Jr. teamed up with Andy Pilgrim and Kelly Collins for the Rolex 24 Hours of Daytona and finished fourth. Afterward, Dale Jr. admitted that there's a difference between being his dad's employee and his teammate.

"He expects a lot from me as a driver for his Winston Cup team, but he expects even more from me now because I'm his teammate," Dale Jr. said. "Now I know what Mike Skinner has been going through. Dad's such a competitor."

But it was in Dale Sr.'s final race that he did what some thought was out of character for the fiercely competitive, win-at-all-costs Intimidator. Running third on the final lap, Earnhardt decided not to go for the win. Instead, he chose to keep the rest of the field at bay and let his son and Waltrip fight it out for the

Now, Dale Jr. must somehow find the strength to go on racing without the man who taught him.

victory while he protected them from the contenders in pursuit.

Seconds later, he was dead. And while the son will face the challenges of replacing his legendary father in the years ahead, even if he manages to win seven Cup titles like his dad did, it won't be the same without him.

"The highlight of my life is seeing the smile on my daddy's face," Earnhardt Jr. once said. "I mean, that is what this is all about: Making people happy. It does my heart good to know how happy he is, how happy my team is." ∎

Dale Sr. said that racing and being together brought him closer to his son.

Where Legends are Made

Nothing else matches the tradition, spectacle

By Roland Lazenby

Among the sad facts to emerge from Dale Earnhardt's final lap is this: The legend of Daytona International Speedway only grows. Nothing can diminish it.

Not even tragedy.

"Daytona is Daytona. It's the first race; it's the biggest race," explains Eddie Wood, part owner of the Wood Brothers Racing team that's won 11 races at Daytona over the years. "It's the Super Bowl of racing."

Winning there brings the biggest rewards in racing, which means that winning there demands the biggest risks in all of racing. Always has. Always will.

Yet never again will a driver execute a draft move in the final lap of the Daytona 500 without bringing to mind both Earnhardt's demise and his fierce aggressiveness. Now they are a permanent part of a Daytona character that is rich and deep and troubling and majestic. Over the years, fans and competitors at the 2.5-mile track have seen it all, the great moments, the heart-spinning finishes, all mixed with the range of setbacks and losses that life on

# of Daytona

Above, David Pearson holds the Daytona trophy after his 1976 victory. At left, the engine on Curtis Turner's 1966 Chevy blows up during the 1967 race.

Where
Legends
are
Made

the NASCAR circuit brings — the untimely deaths of loved ones and close friends, the smashed cars and fractured plans, the off-track battles for drivers and sponsors.

Few have seen more than Glen Wood, the patriarch of the Wood Brothers clan. Wood's personal history spans the explosive growth of stock-car racing, beginning on the dirt tracks of the South just after World War II and running through the modern boom of big-time NASCAR competition.

Of the Woods' many victories, some the greatest have come at Daytona. They first won on the big track in 1963 in a freakish turn of events. In the days leading up to the race, the Woods' hopes seemed dashed when their qualifying driver, Marvin Panch, was badly injured in a preliminary race.

Panch was pulled from a fiery crash by another lesser-known driver, Tiny Lund. Deeply grateful, Panch asked the Woods to reward Lund's lifesaving efforts by letting him drive their Ford in the Daytona showcase. The Woods

The Daytona 500 is the Super Bowl of racing

agreed, and Lund responded by pulling off a major upset and winning the race.

That 1963 Daytona finish is considered the event that established Ford as a top competitor in stock-car racing.

Asked for his favorite Daytona memory, the elder Wood cites his team's 1976 victory, often described as the most exciting finish in the track's illustrious history. I've never quite had a feeling of excitement like I did that day," Glen Wood said.

The Wood Brothers' Mercury, driven by David Pearson, had battled Richard Petty through most of the race. From the pits, Eddie Wood kept contact with Pearson on the radio. "Richard and David had been going at each other all day long," Eddie recalled. "It was just those two. On the radio, Pearson told me, 'We'll go down to the last lap and have it out.' And that's how it happened.

"As they came off of Turn 2 in the last lap, David said, 'I don't know if I can get him or not.' Then, as he got to Turn 3, he told me, 'I got him.' "

But at Turn 4, Petty attempted to push past Pearson and bumped him cutting back in. Both cars spun out just yards short of the finish line. Petty's car died, but somehow Pearson kept the Mercury Cyclone alive. Frantically, the Petty crew tried to push his car across the line. ➜

Richard Petty was a winner in 1971 (top right), but not so lucky in '75.

Where Legends are Made

The collision, meanwhile, had left Pearson a bit disoriented; he couldn't see Petty's car. "Has he crossed the line?" Pearson yelled over the radio. "No," Eddie Wood yelled back through the radio.

"Well, I'm coming," Pearson said and gunned the Cyclone over the line to the Woods' biggest win.

Like the Woods, most competitors in racing count their victories at Daytona as their most cherished. And often most controversial, because of the daring required.

Take for example Jeff Gordon's big move in 1999 to edge Earnhardt and win the 500 for the second time in three years.

"With the camera angle that they had on that, it really looked a lot closer than it actually was," Gordon recalled. Rusty Wallace had the lead late until Gordon made a daring pass, which left Wallace fussing.

Daytona's character is rich, deep, troubling and majestic

"We all made a bunch out of it at that particular time," Wallace recalled. "The fans did, I did and whatever. You look back at it right now and it's no big deal."

Bobby Hamilton crashed in the backstretch of Lap 175 of the 200-lap race which brought out a caution and set up the turn of events. Wallace and teammate Jeremy Mayfield, whose Fords had been running first and second when Hamilton crashed, chose not to pit for fuel and tires, but Gordon and the other contenders did. Then they lined up behind Wallace and Mayfield for the 22 laps remaining.

Mayfield soon lost ground, but Wallace held on until he pulled the lead draft toward Turn 1 on Lap 190.

That's when Gordon headed his Chevy for the low side of the track to make a move for the lead. He crossed the yellow line marks at pit road's exit, almost hit Ricky Rudd's Ford as it was coming back onto the track, and still managed to pass Wallace. Once he got the lead, Gordon never gave it up.

"It certainly was an exciting move, but when you're going for a Daytona 500 win, you've got to make moves like that sometimes," Gordon said. "It's just kind of the way drafting works at Daytona and when you get momentum, you've got to take advantage of that momentum.

"If you're talking about coming down with a few laps to ➡

Pete Hamilton and Sharon Brown celebrate Hamilton's Daytona win in 1970.

go, then you're going to take some risks. I certainly wouldn't make a move like that 10 laps into the race, but I'm certainly going to do it again if I had to near the end."

"I think it was definitely a daring move," Mayfield said. "But I don't think Gordon would have done anything to jeopardize anybody. I mean if he knew that he couldn't make it or it was really going to be a really high risk, he wouldn't have done it."

"It's a move that's worked for me several times and it's probably the only place on the race track where you can do something like that," Gordon said of the low side of Turn 1. "Of course I wasn't expecting Ricky Rudd to be there, either. It would have been a perfect plan had he not been there, but because he was it made things a little hairy. Luckily, he got out of the way and I made it through there all right."

Winning at Daytona brings the biggest risks in racing

The low side of Turn 1 was also where Gordon dove to pass Bill Elliott for the lead late in the 1997 Daytona 500. Gordon took the low path while Hendrick Motorsports teammates Terry Labonte and Ricky Craven went outside around Elliott's Ford. Mayfield wound up 20th after his flat tire but was still close enough to the front to have a good view of Gordon's pass of Wallace.

Dale Jarrett has three career wins in NASCAR'S biggest race, the last coming in 2000 when he passed Johnny Benson with four laps to go.

"When I got involved in Winston Cup racing I had the dream that everybody else does of one day being in that Victory Lane and having a Daytona 500 trophy," Jarrett told the media afterward.

Only Richard Petty and Cale Yarborough, with four Daytona 500 victories, have now won the event more than Jarrett and Bobby Allison, who also won the race three times.

Jarrett's 2000 victory celebration also was marked by an on-track confrontation from Martin, upset by Jarrett's manuevers on Lap 187 as they fought to move past Benson's Pontiac.

"Mark had radioed and asked if he went high would I go with him, and I said yes," Jarrett explained. "We tried it the lap before and didn't get a very good run. Nothing else ➜

Bill Elliott and his wife, Martha, hoisted the trophy in 1985.

Where
Legends
are
Made

was said then. We came down through the trioval the next time, went into Turn 1, Mark went high and I went into the corner high with every intention of going with Mark."

But Jarrett saw Burton going low and went for the opportunity.

"I've got to protect my position at that point," Jarrett said. "I didn't lie to Mark Martin. I know he felt like that and there's nothing I can say that's going to change his mind. But when I looked up and saw the 99 (Burton) knowing he had the 94 (Elliott) right behind him, I was getting ready to lose my spot for sure."

After getting past Martin, Jarrett still had Benson to deal with. "I knew that he was going to try to block me," Jarrett said. "I faked high and he went up there, and as soon as I saw him move up the race track I cut my car dead left. I was committed. If I would have had to go to the apron, which I almost had to, that's where I was going."

The Daytona 500 is a complex mix of victory, heart-spinning finishes, setbacks and tragedy

Although his success at the 500 was limited to his one victory, Earnhardt himself loved the Daytona speedway, loved the demands it placed on his talent and that of other drivers.

He last won there in the International Race of Champions series in 2000. "I'm 48 and moving," Earnhardt said at the time. "I have a lot of racing yet before I quit or slow down. To win a race of cars built as equally as they can be built and with drivers that are champions. You race against a lot of wins and a lot of championships, and it makes you feel good to be competitive in that kind of racing and even win it.

"Winning it here at Daytona makes it even more so for me because this is a race track I love to race at."

Now that Earnhardt fire is inextricably linked with Daytona. And the legacy deepens. ∎

Driver's last prayer was for safety, wisdom preacher says

By ALLEN G. BREED
Associated Press

RALEIGH, N.C. — Most race day Sundays for the past 13 years, the Rev. Max Helton has stood at the side of Dale Earnhardt's black No. 3 Chevy and led a prayer.

Sunday's Daytona 500 was no exception — Earnhardt insisted on it.

Helton said he gathered on the track with Earnhardt's wife, Teresa, and Richard Childress, the car's owner.

"We held hands through his window," said Helton, a Presbyterian minister and founder of Motor Racing Outreach.

"He says, 'Just pray that I'll be wise in putting the car at the right place at the right time ... and be able to drive with wisdom.' And we did pray about that. And we did pray for safety."

Racing fans feel a giant void

Towns built around racing show their respect for one of NASCAR's greatest drivers.

By JENNA FRYER
The Associated Press

MOORESVILLE, N.C. — A single black balloon broke free from the wrought iron fence surrounding the sprawling complex housing Dale Earnhardt's racing teams.

A security guard caught the balloon and retied it next to the growing memorial of personalized tributes left by fans Monday in memory of the seven-time Winston Cup champion who died the day before in a crash at the Daytona 500.

A sign said the compound was "respectfully closed today." Still, employees of Dale Earnhardt Inc. solemnly filed in, past the security officers posted at every gate.

"It ain't too good in there. Everyone's trying their best," said Cam Ramey, the security chief.

Dale Earnhardt Jr., who finished second in Sunday's race, emerged from the complex shortly before noon in a black pickup truck. He was driven across the street and up a private drive to his home.

"He's holding up as best he can under the circumstances," said Steve Crisp, who drove Earnhardt Jr. to his house.

"There is a lot of character in that family and in that organization," said H.A. "Humpy" Wheeler, president of Lowe's Motor Speedway in nearby Concord.

He said he thought the teams still would participate in this weekend's Dura-Lube 400 at North Carolina Speedway in Rockingham.

Hundreds of fans left poems, letters and pictures at the compound, quietly taking in the scene, occasionally wiping away a tear. "Forever A Champion," one sign said.

When a team wins a race, tradition at Dale Earnhardt Inc. calls for a checkered flag to fly in front of the complex until the next race begins the following week. On Monday, the flag was at half-staff, representing both Michael Waltrip's victory at Daytona and Earnhardt's death on the last lap of the race.

"It's like Superman is dead," said Craig Freshwater, who made the 30-mile trip from Charlotte to pay his respects. "Heroes aren't supposed to die."

"He was a guy you either loved or loved to hate," said Earnhardt fan Gary Farabee. "But it's just not the same this morning. It just doesn't feel right.

"Over the last year, I think he exposed his inner self, his softer side, a little more," Farabee said. "I don't think I pulled for him as much as a racer as I pulled for him as a man."

When Earnhardt finished, he squeezed Helton's hand, as he always did. But this time, something was different.

"I noticed it at that particular time, that he seemed to squeeze my hand a little longer than he normally does," Helton said in a telephone interview Wednesday.

After the race, Helton was in a prayer circle with the same people. Only this time it was at a hospital, and his old friend was dead.

"No one expected, I think, Dale Earnhardt to die in a race car," he said. "Maybe in a plane crash, maybe in some other way; but not in a race car. Because he was so good and he's been through so many crashes and walked away from them that seemed a lot worse than the one he was in and which took his life."

Helton, whose ministry has traveled the NASCAR circuit since 1988, said he didn't think much about Earnhardt's gesture at the time, because The Intimidator was always surprising him. He remembers one instance when he greeted Earnhardt in the victory circle.

"Man, he grabbed me by the neck and pulled my head in and said, 'Let's pray and thank God for this victory,'" Helton recalled. "He was just that way."

Helton was waiting in the victory circle Sunday and watching the race on a Jumbotron when the accident occurred. But he didn't think it

looked "that horribly bad" and went to congratulate winner Michael Waltrip.

Helton was walking casually through the garage when someone told him it was serious. He was ushered into a waiting police car and rushed to nearby Halifax Medical Center.

"They were still working on him at the time, and I was there with them when the doctors told them, 'Listen, we've done everything we can do,'" Helton said. "I was right there by his side at the table in the trauma room."

Helton led Teresa Earnhardt, Dale Jr. and Childress in a prayer beside the trauma table.

"We were praying that God would give sustaining grace and that God would give his strength and wisdom," he said. "We were really hurting, and we talked about in our prayer, even confessed the fact that, yes, we're really hurt and we're deeply saddened by this, and we're asking for God's saving grace through this."

Helton said some might think it odd that Earnhardt's final prayer for safety would be answered with a fatal wreck. But he doesn't see it that way.

"If you look at that, I mean, God really watched over him and cared for him, because he took him on," he said. "You know, that's the ultimate safety. He'll never hurt again."

Festive Daytona scene turns sour

AP/Wide World Photos

DAYTONA BEACH, Fla. — Inside the museum next to the track where Dale Earnhardt died, roses started piling up on top of a black Monte Carlo pace car that looks hauntingly like The Intimidator's.

In restaurants across the street, patrons left suddenly when they heard the news.

The city of Daytona Beach, normally home to a rowdy, drunken Mardi Gras scene after the Daytona 500, fell into mourning Sunday night after hearing one of auto racing's greats had been killed in a crash on the final lap.

"I can't stop crying," said Patty Miesel, a race fan from Pittsburgh. "I've been crying ever since I heard the news. We love all of the NASCAR drivers, but Earnhardt had a special place in our heart."

She and her husband went to a souvenir shop after they heard the news and had a special T-shirt made. It has a big No. 3 on it and the words, "Winners come and go, but legends live forever."

Colleagues of The Intimidator — as Earnhardt was known far and wide — were equally shocked.

"No matter where it happens or how it happens or even how prepared you think you might be for it, losing somebody close to you hurts," said Kyle Petty, whose son Adam died last year in a wreck. "My heart just breaks for the family."

Petty's teammate, John Andretti, added: "I feel like somebody kicked me in the chest. I'm stunned. And I'm really sad. That's about all I can say."

Race fan Ken Satherfield of South Carolina fought the traffic and made his way 30 miles up Interstate 95. When he heard the news, he turned back to join a troupe of fans for a vigil near Daytona International Speedway.

"We were really affected by this," Satherfield said. "We were very big Earnhardt fans."

Flags at the track and throughout the city were lowered to half-staff, as disbelief faded into teary-eyed acceptance.

"You never think anyone will get killed, but he was the last one you'd think that would happen to," said former NASCAR champion Ned Jarrett, wiping away tears.

He wasn't the only one who had trouble believing it had happened.

"After the race was over, I heard things didn't look very good," driver Jeremy Mayfield said. "But, man, Earnhardt? You figure he'll bounce right back. Your first thought is, 'Hey, he'll probably come back next week at Rockingham and beat us all.'"

Race fans Philip and Nancy Geraci of Massachusetts also turned back toward the speedway when they heard the news. Making their way back to the track to reminisce, they saw Earnhardt's trailer move down International Speedway Boulevard, with a police escort.

"It seemed like a funeral procession," Nancy Geraci said.

Reid Pelletier of Danbury, Conn., had just finished dinner when the news spread across the restaurant. People started crying. Some simply stopped eating and walked out.

Pelletier left and started driving toward the track. He was in his car and didn't plan to get out for a while.

"I'm emotionally shaken and in shock," he said. "I don't want to go to sleep now."

Earnhardt's legacy
will remain

By Mike Morris
Associated Press

"Dale, with us always."

That sign outside Daytona International Speedway speaks of the continuing love affair stock car racing has with Dale Earnhardt.

He was killed Sunday, one fateful corner away from another great afternoon at his favorite racetrack, dying from head injuries in a wreck on the last turn of the last lap of the Daytona 500.

The Intimidator won 34 times on Daytona's 2-mile oval, although it wasn't always easy.

For the first 19 years that he came to the sprawling track built by NASCAR founder Bill France Sr., he won nearly everything — the July Winston Cup race, qualifying races, Busch and IROC races.

Everything but the Daytona 500 — losing once when he blew a tire after dominating the race for 499 miles.

That finally changed in 1998, when Earnhardt gleefully took the checkered flag in NASCAR's Super Bowl — punching his left fist out the window of his famed black No. 3 Chevrolet in triumph and spinning through the grass in a personal victory celebration.

As he drove slowly down pit lane toward Victory Circle, his smile gleaming beneath his bushy mustache, rival crews lined his path, slapping his palm and giving him thumbs up for what might have been the most awaited victory in NASCAR history.

Afterward, he showed a soft side that few knew he possessed.

"This one meant the world to me," Earnhardt said, his eyes shining. "People may think I'm tough and I don't care — and I am tough — but I'm human, too. I want to win every time I go out there, but there's some races that mean more than others. This is one of them."

Fans were rarely ambivalent about Earnhardt. Millions loved the dashing, cowboylike figure. Millions more vilified "The Man in Black."

Even more than his record-tying seven Winston Cup championships and his 76 victories — sixth all-time and the most among current drivers — Earnhardt's legacy is the role he played in NASCAR's rise to the mainstream of American culture.

His father, Ralph, was a rough and tumble stock car pioneer, never afraid of a fight — on or off the track.

The elder Earnhardt died of a heart attack while working on a race car in the garage of his North Carolina home. The 1956 NASCAR Sportsman division champion was 45.

Dale, 22 at the time, desperately wanted to follow his father into racing but had few resources. With only a ninth-grade education, he was working in a textile factory and twice divorced with three children by the age of 25.

What he had in abundance was an aggressive confidence that eventually translated to rides and racing victories.

Once he reached the top level of NASCAR for good, Earnhardt was an instant success, winning the Rookie of the Year title in 1979 and the first of his championships in 1980.

His racing prowess earned him millions of dollars on the track and many millions more from souvenir and memorabilia sales that dwarf those of his racing rivals.

"Image is everything," said Don Hawk, Earnhardt's former business manager. "People perceived Dale Earnhardt in different ways, good and bad. But they are always aware of him and care what he does, and they want a piece of him."

AP/Wide World Photos

The success brought Earnhardt a lush, if hectic, lifestyle.

He flew to races, personal appearances and hunting and fishing trips in a private jet, occasionally relaxed aboard a 100-foot yacht, aptly christened "Sunday Money," and loved working around his 400-acre North Carolina farm, keeping an eye on the black Angus cattle, commercial chicken houses and quarterhorses when he had the chance.

He married Teresa Hunter in 1982, and added daughter Taylor to a family that already included daughter Kelly and sons Kerry and Dale Jr. from his previous marriages.

"He wasn't around a whole lot when I was growing up because he was off racing most of the time," Dale Jr. said. "But I always knew he cared about me and the other kids. He let us know in his way."

He owned a Chevrolet dealership and, although he continued to drive for longtime friend Richard Childress, Earnhardt decided to start his

own team, Dale Earnhardt Inc.

After starting with a Busch series program and a few Winston Cup races in 1997, the team moved Steve Park into NASCAR's top series in 1998, brought Dale Jr. in as his teammate in 2000 and added Michael Waltrip, the Daytona winner, as a third driver this season.

Earnhardt also was helping Kerry get his racing career into gear. But the arrival as a star of Dale Jr. — who won two straight Busch championships then two Winston Cup races as a rookie — particularly delighted him.

Dale Jr.'s success coincided with his father's resurgence as a title contender after a dry spell that had some wondering if his racing skills had declined.

At an age when most drivers talk about their accomplishments, the 49-tear-old Earnhardt was confident he could win a record eighth title.

"Racing has been pretty much my whole life," Earnhardt said in a recent interview. "We're building something here, and my boys are here.

"I'm going to be racing for a while yet, but when the time comes, this is going to be what I do, run this team and stay involved in the sport."

It's true he's gone now. But his legacy won't leave any time soon.

Dale Earnhardt's
LEGACY

AP/Wide World Photos

1951: Born in Kannapolis.

1973: Earnhardt's father, Ralph, dies at age 45 of a heart attack while working on a race car.

1975: Earnhardt makes his Winston Cup debut in the World 600 at Charlotte Motor Speedway. He started 33rd and finished 22nd in a Dodge owned by Ed Negre. He earned $2,245 and finished one spot ahead of his future boss, Richard Childress.

1979: He wins the Winston Cup Rookie of the Year title while driving for Rod Osterlund, the season that includes his first victory at Bristol.

1980: Earnhardt wins five races en route to his first Winston Cup championship. He's the only driver to win a series championship after being Rookie of the Year.

1981: Earnhardt struggles, failing to win a race or a pole. Osterlund sells the team in mid-season and Earnhardt quits. He drives for Childress the rest of the season.

1982: He joins Bud Moore's team. He wins at Darlington in April but fractures a knee in a crash at Talladega. He doesn't miss a race.

1983: He wins two races before bolting back to a car owned by Childress, with whom he'd spend the rest of racing career.

1984: He wins two races including one at Atlanta where newcomer Terry Schoonover is killed. "I'm sorry it happened, real sorry," Earnhardt said. "It's something you don't want to think about happening, and I try not to."

AP/Wide World Photos

1985: Earnhardt wins four races and finishes eighth in the season points race.

1986: He wins his second Winston Cup title with five victories.

1987: Earnhardt wins a third series title with 11 victories.

1989: He finishes second in the series, losing to Rusty Wallace by 12 points.

1990: Earnhardt earns a then-record $3 million in prize money while taking home a fourth Winston Cup title, 26 points ahead of Mark Martin.

1991: He takes a fifth series title.

1992: He finishes 12th in the season's points race, tying his worst showing of his Winston Cup career.

1993: Earnhardt wins a sixth Winston Cup championship.

1994: He ties Richard Petty's mark of seven Winston Cup titles.

1997: Earnhardt goes winless for the first time since 1981.

1998: He claims his only Daytona 500 victory, in his 20th attempt.

2000: He finishes second in the points race to Bobby Labonte. He wins his last race in October at Talladega, Ala., giving him 76 career victories.

2001: Earnhardt is killed in a crash during the last lap of the Daytona 500, while a car he owns, driven by Michael Waltrip, wins the race.

The sport **speaks out** on its lost legend

THE ASSOCIATED PRESS

Reaction to Dale Earnhardt's death Sunday in a crash on the last turn of the last lap of the Daytona 500:

* * *

"My heart is hurting right now. I would rather be any place right this moment than here. It's so painful." —race winner Michael Waltrip at his press conference. Waltrip drove a car owned by Earnhardt.

the last one you'd think that would happen to.

"He had a tremendous impact on NASCAR racing. He's done so much to help the sport get where it is today. He took the sport to new places. It's going to hard for anyone else to take it there. He leaves a big, big void here that will be very hard to fill."—Ned Jarrett, broadcaster, former driver and father of driver Dale Jarrett.

* * *

"We're going to have to take a look at some of the safety issues. My driver tested the HANS (Head And Neck Safety) device over the summer and he will not get in the car without it now. If Dale had that on, we'd probably be looking at a different situation."—Todd Parrott, Dale Jarrett's crew chief.

* * *

"I feel like somebody kicked me in the chest. I'm stunned. And I'm really sad. That's about all I can say."—driver John Andretti.

* * *

"Like so many people around the world, I became a NASCAR fan because I became a Dale Earnhardt fan. Dale was someone I was proud to have my son look up to. We all have our memories we will cherish, memories of excitement, competitiveness and most of all memories of a great man. On behalf of the people of Alabama, I extend my thoughts and prayers to his family and friends."—Alabama Gov. Don Siegelman.

* * *

"Like many others, we were fans of Dale Earnhardt — certainly the driver, but especially the man. In spite of our intense rivalry, Dale Earnhardt has been a great friend to us and to all who have helped to make this sport great. Dale Earnhardt transcended NASCAR. His loss will have an effect on racing and its fans worldwide."—Dan Davis, director of Ford Racing Technology.

introduced him, he got the biggest applause there. He's the man, he is NASCAR Winston Cup racing. We haven't had something like this happen. We've got a lot of work to do at the track in the next three weeks (for the March 11 Cracker Barrel 400), but I don't feel like doing anything. I'm just numb. I've lost a great friend."-Ed Clark, president of Atlanta Motor Speedway.

* * *

"Dale Earnhardt was the greatest race car driver that ever lived. He could do things with a race car that no one else could. You never think anyone will get killed, but he was

now. I didn't see much of what happened. After the race was over, I heard things didn't look very good but, man, Earnhardt. You figure he'll bounce right back. Your first thought is, hey, he'll probably come back next week at Rockingham and beat us all."—driver Jeremy Mayfield.

* * *

"It's just the way this sport is. That's the chances you take. It's unfortunate it happened to him. It just don't seem right. It's hard to believe. You don't think things like that will happen to drivers of his caliber.